The Business
of Good Government

The Business of Good Government is a nativity
play written for performance in 1960 in the
church of Brent Knoll, in Somerset: most of
the original cast had never acted before.
This proved to be the first of a series of vivid
and effective experiments in community
drama in which the playwright, John Arden,
has collaborated with his wife, Margaretta
D'Arcy, the actress. It has now been adapted
to suit any kind of production and John
Arden's notes contain suggestions for costumes, properties and the singing of the
music.

Plays by John Arden

Serjeant Musgrave's Dance
The Waters of Babylon
Live Like Pigs
The Happy Haven
The Workhouse Donkey
Ironhand
(adapted from Goethe's *Goetz von Berlichingen*)
Left-handed Liberty
Armstrong's Last Goodnight
Soldier, Soldier and other plays

*

by John Arden and Margaretta D'Arcy

The Royal Pardon

The Business
of Good Government

A CHRISTMAS PLAY

BY

JOHN ARDEN AND

MARGARETTA D'ARCY

LONDON

METHUEN & CO LTD

11 NEW FETTER LANE

First published 1963
Reprinted 1965 and 1967
© 1963 by John Arden
Printed in Great Britain by
Butler & Tanner Ltd
Frome and London
Cat. No. 02/2668/24 (hardbound)
02/6303/24 (paperback)

Preface
and Production Notes

There is a great deal of amateur drama in Britain today, but in far too many cases it does not contribute as fully as it might to the general life around it. The performance of plays is an activity that should come as naturally as preparing a meal, eating it, singing, dancing, kissing or football. It should not be associated with snobbishness, superior education, improved accents, and an enviable knowledge of 'what they do in London'. Nor should it merely be a means of extinguishing the provincial professional theatre by feeble imitations of its slicker successes. Amateur and professional must respect each other's work – complementing one another, rather than competing.

When I was asked to write this short play for performance in a village church at Christmas, I had not directly written for amateurs before. On assembling a cast, we found that the majority had never acted, and indeed had only turned up at all under pressure from the Vicar – who had apparently reassured one or two doubtful volunteers by promising that they would not be expected to *act*, merely to speak the lines as though Reading the Lesson. It was therefore essential that they should not be frightened away by the thought of having to 'build a character' in the Stanislavski sense – we concentrated instead on bringing out the meaning of their lines until, without entirely realizing it, they created from their own personalities a character, completely natural, belonging both to their own experience and to the world of the play. As rehearsals progressed I found that my lines were undergoing a number of changes – the actors' normal habits of speech reasserted themselves wherever the writing had fallen into awkwardness and pretentious phraseology, and a kind of gentle erosion of these difficult places produced in the end a simpler and stronger text than that with which we had begun.

This was all to the good: for I felt that the one thing to avoid was any sense that the actors were puppets in the hands of author or producer – if the play was to be a communal expression of Christmas, then everyone who took part in it must be able to bring his own personal contribution to the whole. The producer's main business was to work these contributions together until a satisfactory unity resulted, rather than to pre-conceive such a unity and then force everyone else to fit themselves into it.

In the same way, I allowed the structural features of the fifteenth-century church to impose a basic shape upon the action – the play was written to take place within the architec-ture, unhindered by any sort of artificial scenery. The costumes were not designed in any detail: rather were they improvised from such materials and garments as could be lent by members of the cast and their friends. A hazardous technique, of course – if it goes wrong you can find yourself with a production looking like a badly-hung clothes-line on a March morning, and it is necessary to start with at least a general outline scheme of colours and textures – but it does enable the actors to dress themselves to suit both their own characters and the parts they are playing. They can wear a skeleton of the costume from the beginning of rehearsals, modifying it where it seems best, until it becomes an integral part of their performance. If costumes are hired or even specially made up from a series of designs, they are not likely to be ready until near the opening night; the actors have no time to feel at home in them; and any 'amateurishness' in their performance becomes the more pronounced in comparison with the 'professionalism' of their clothing.

In this printed text I have had to provide stage directions to suit any production in any auditorium, and I have been asked to give some indication of costumes, properties and décor. But with this sort of play there is no substitute for imaginative improvisation to suit local conditions. All these notes are to be taken as suggestions only, to be followed or ignored as circumstances direct. This also applies to the text itself. Casting requirements may make nonsense of some of the characters. There is no reason why the Shepherds should always have to speak in west-country rhythms. The Midwife and the Hostess could perhaps be amalgamated into one character. If Joseph has no voice for singing, his song could be spoken. At Brent Knoll, two of the Wise Men and Herod's Secretary had to be played by women. I have suggested that the Wise Men have an Attendant each—at Brent Knoll these were played by children which gave an implication of Oriental pomp to the visit: but in a production where all the actors are children this point would perhaps not so easily be made. Generally speaking, there are no fixed rules governing such improvisations and variations – Bertolt Brecht has said 'If it works, it works' – the one essential condition is that the meaning of the play should never be obscured. The rest is a matter of taste and of adaptation to local circumstance.

Details of Staging

I have assumed for the purpose of the stage directions that the play is to be presented in a long hall with a stage across one end of it – the usual form for village halls, community centres, youth clubs, school speech halls, and so on. I have further assumed that this hall has the minimum of theatrical conveniences and that the stage is connected to the 'backstage area' by only one door. If the play can work under such conditions, then there will be no difficulty in preparing a production for a better-equipped auditorium. In a hall containing an open stage or an arena stage or any other of the more traditional forms – which are now being revived here and there after a century or so of neglect – some modification of my directions may be found necessary. But on the whole this sort of stage will be greatly to the advantage of the play: indeed I recommend that where a proscenium stage is to be used the producer should

start by removing the proscenium frame, curtains, and foot-
lights. Overhead battens of lights should be retained, but will
look much better if they can be denuded of those little blue
cutlet-frills, which on most amateur stages are used to conceal
them from the eyes of the audience. Wings and backcloths are
not necessary unless the rear wall of the stage is visually so
disturbing as to require some covering – I would not suggest
that a radiator or a batch of fuse-boxes be kept in full view
throughout the action.

On the other hand, it is essential to the structure of the play
that the actors *are* seen, on the stage, waiting their cues, from
beginning to end. They come in, in procession, and go out at
the end in the same manner. The only exceptions are the Holy
Family, who arrive in the middle, and then flee to Egypt; and
the Wise Men, who flee to Persia. The Wise Men's Attendants
may perhaps wait for their entry until the scene of the Epiph-
any: but this is only a device for preventing the stage becoming
too cluttered, and if there is room, they can be with their
masters from the beginning. I have indicated on the sketch the
positioning of characters which has governed my stage directions – this is, of course, no more than a guide. The pulpit need
not be a very elaborate pulpit – a small reading desk would
do – or if the space is particularly cramped, the Angel could
simply stand or sit at the corner of the stage. The Angel can
also be the prompter – where there are no wings or curtains a
separate prompter will be awkward to arrange – and he can
have a large Bible with the text of the play inserted. Some of
the Angel's speeches, in fact, are best delivered as though read
directly from the Bible. The other characters should have
unassuming chairs to sit on – the chairs must appear to be the
furniture of the stage rather than fittings in, say, Herod's
palace or the Bethlehem inn – and when they are not taking
part in the action they wait for their cues in a relaxed and
natural way.

In front of the chairs the acting area should be completely

clear of furniture or steps and should be as wide and deep as possible. There should be steps between the audience and the stage so positioned that entrances and exits can be made with the minimum of fuss. At the rear of the acting area I have indicated a 'rostrum', which need only be one or two steps high, and which serves to distance Mary from the rest of the play at the time of the Birth. If it is felt that the stage needs some sort of backcloth, this could be a patterned hanging or perhaps a pictorial design with a stylized representation of the Crucifixion behind the rostrum. The Wise Men and Shepherds are shown as sitting in front of the stage at an intermediate level. I do not think they need do this unless the stage is very small: but so many stages *are*, that it is as well to be prepared. Otherwise they can be on-stage, well forward, at the same respective corners – the Shepherds in front of the pulpit. The spare seat used for the accommodation of Mary after the Birth of Jesus, can be left behind the pulpit until it is required.

Lighting should be simple. The scenes are all very short; some of them take place in deliberately unfixed locations and night and day alternate in an inconsistent manner: so clearly any attempt to light the play naturalistically will not work. At Brent Knoll we lit the acting area very strongly with two or three white floods and that was all. But there the arches of the church produced their own dramatic shadows, and in an architecturally uninteresting hall something more imaginative might be thought to be called for.*

Costumes

This play is not historically accurate, nor is it entirely a

---

* I have said nothing special about productions in churches: but these should not involve many extra difficulties. The altar will provide a focal point for the action; the Angel can use the real pulpit or reading-desk; and, where they are conveniently arranged, the choir stalls can accommodate the actors between their scenes. The chancel steps of most churches provide a natural open stage, as we found very happily at Brent Knoll.

'modernization' of the story. It is a straightforward narration of the events given in the Gospels, with incidental references backwards to ancient Judaea and forwards to the twentieth-century, wherever I have thought appropriate. The play is 'realist' in that the characters stand for themselves as Shepherds, Wise Men, Kings and what have you, and are not intended to carry symbolical or psychological overtones. But it is also 'non-realist' in that the principal action is miraculous and accepted as such. This double level of interpretation should be reflected in the appearance of the characters. I do not think that true historical costume or straightforward modern dress would be entirely satisfactory: what is required is that each individual character should appear to be the *essence* of that person, from whatever period the details of his costume be drawn.

Thus at Brent Knoll: *Herod* wore the robes and crown of a medieval king over a gold-embroidered jacket and black trousers; his *Secretary* wore a gold high-necked Chinese dressing-gown and a small round black cap; the *Wise Men* were dressed in long tunics and mantles – two of them made-up in a Japanese style and wearing heavy hats of fur like Tartars, the third made-up like an African and wearing a jewelled head-band; the *Shepherds* wore pretty much what shepherds wear in Somerset today, though the old man had an old-fashioned smock-frock, and they all wore blankets round their shoulders; the *Midwife*, *Hostess*, and *Farm-Girl* were dressed like Flemish peasant-women in Brueghel's paintings, with long skirts, aprons, and head-kerchiefs; *Joseph* wore a heavy blanket cloak over a coarse jersey, trousers tucked into wellington boots, and fur cap; *Mary* wore a dark blue cloak over a long red dress, much as she is traditionally shown in paintings; and the *Angel* wore an all-enveloping black mantle with a touch of white shirt-collar at his neck.* As I have already said, these costumes

---

* N.B. The Angel in this play is not only a Divine Messenger, but also the Presenter of the Play, the Prompter, Herod's conscience, a

arose to some extent from what was available to us, and another production might make use of an entirely different range of garments, no less suitable.

I would emphasize, however, that no one in the play wore a wig or a false beard, and that no make-up was used except for the Wise Men (who were deliberately exotic in appearance), and except where rendered absolutely necessary by the quality of the lighting. If actors who have little or no experience of the stage appear at any point to be 'constructing' a character beyond the extent of their own experience, the falsity will immediately be felt. Therefore, producers working with local amateur players should not be afraid of adjusting the ages of characters given in my directions. If there is no old man to play the Old Shepherd, then it is better to present him as a middle-aged Shepherd, and so on. (Obviously, for school or youth-group productions this does not apply).

Properties

The best rule to be followed about properties is 'If in doubt, cut them out'. There are a few which are essential – a Baby for Mary (which will have to be concealed somewhere very cunningly at the rear of the stage, for her to bring out at the right moment without the audience noticing); documents for Herod's Secretary, the Wise Men, and Joseph; gifts for the Wise Men; a broom for the Hostess; a corn-sack for the Farm-Girl; crooks and a flask or firkin for the Shepherds. In the Brent Knoll production Herod carried an orb and sceptre at the beginning of the play, and later produced a large sword on the line 'It is fitting that the honour of one man should die for the good of the people'. It was with this sword that he terrified the Farm-Girl, and it seemed a useful

---

kind of Devil, and a Palace Official. So, however he is dressed, he will only work dramatically if he has an interesting and unpretentious human personality. Under no circumstances should he be equipped with a halo, wings, and long golden locks.

accompaniment to his acceptance of the Massacre; but had he not been wearing a crown and wide robes it would have been less appropriate. If the Wise Men have no Attendants, they will have to have some satchels or purses for the carriage of their gifts. Joseph might have a walking-staff and the Midwife a napkin or towel. The Shepherds might have a brazier to warm themselves at: though I fancy this could cause more problems than it would solve. The Angel needs his Bible.

All these properties must be attractive objects in their own right. They must look as though they are really used – just as the costumes must look as though they are really worn. Unless the actors can obtain a sensual pleasure from the handling of their properties and the wearing of their clothes, they will never be able to act naturally with them, and the audience will remain unconvinced of the reality of the story.

Music

The songs sung in the course of the play will all fit existing and easily available tunes. The three carols –

> 'I saw three ships'
> 'As Joseph was a-walking' (The Cherry Tree Carol)
> 'Down in yon Forest' (The Corpus Christi Carol)

– are medieval in origin and have their own proper melodies. The other songs may be sung to tunes from the *Penguin Book of English Folk Songs* as follows –

> Shepherd's Song, 'I came to town' ('The Grey Cock').
> Shepherd's Lullaby, 'Go to sleep, little baby' ('Long Lankin').
> Farm-Girl's Song, 'The Seed was set' ('John Barleycorn').

The following tune for the remaining song – the Shepherds' Round – was specially composed by Alexander Robertson:*

---

* Reproduced by kind permission of the composer.

Three Part Round by A. Robertson

Who'll lend me six pence   all I want is six pence

To buy a pair of red leather boots   a wide black hat and a new blue jack-et

If you lend him six pence I   swear to you you'll soon regret it

If these tunes are not liked and alternative ones are used, I would recommend that they should be airs of the same basic type, in which the line of music reinforces and emphasizes the meaning of the line of verse, so that the whole thing becomes a single poetic statement rather than a passage of attractive singing with some words vaguely attached.

There is scope in the play for instrumental music, but this should not be used to accompany the songs, except for the processional carols at beginning and end. At Brent Knoll the church organ was used here and also to introduce the first entry of the Shepherds, to accompany the movement of Mary towards the audience after the Birth, and to intensify the sounds of the Massacre of the Innocents.

JOHN ARDEN

the singing is finished, from the pulpit).

ou tidings of great joy, which shall be unto
to God in the highest, and on earth peace,
men.

mes rapidly through the audience.

ll, great joy, peace upon earth – I do not
altogether possible. But it is the business of
ent to try and make them possible.

*up on to the stage the other characters withdraw
though in alarm, and take their seats as quickly
as they may.* HEROD *turns and addresses the*

King. Herod the Great. Ruler of Judaea. To the
oman Empire. To the east, the Persian Empire.
dle, a small country in a very dangerous position.
towards the east, I am afraid of invasion from
I lean towards Rome, then I shall be called upon
ersia. I would prefer to choose neither. But I had
Rome, because Rome rules Egypt, and it is from
at we buy our corn. We are not self-supporting. *I
self-supporting.* I have Roman officers in my army,
advisers in my palace, Roman spies in every depart-
state . . .

SECRETARY *rises from his seat and moves towards
OD. He notices this and immediately changes his tone to
of insincere political rhetoric.*

enormous friendship and generosity shown by the
an people to the people of Judaea can only be repaid by
continued loyalty and vigilance. The historic alliance
een our two great nations must be for every citizen an
nal inspiration. Peace, prosperity, goodwill: one man
ries them all upon his back. If he falls down –

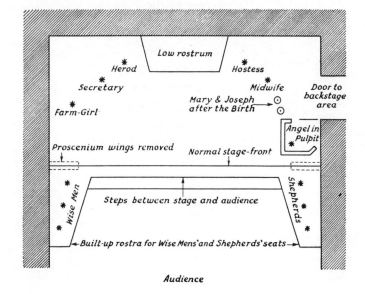

*Sketch showing arrangement of stage
for a typical production in a small hall*

Characters in the Play

ANGEL

KING HEROD

HIS SECRETARY

THREE WISE MEN

THREE ATTENDANTS

THREE SHEPHERDS

HOSTESS OF THE BETHLEHEM INN

JOSEPH

MARY

MIDWIFE

FARM-GIRL

This play was written specially for the village of Brent Knoll in Somerset and was performed there in the Church of St Michael during the Christmas season, 1960. I would like to thank the Vicar of Brent Knoll, the Parish Church Council, and all those who took part in the play or in any way assisted its production.

JOHN ARDEN

The pla
All th
audience

As they ent

I saw
A-sail
I saw t
On Chr

They sail
To Bethle
Saint Mich
Saint John

Joseph did w
Mary did sing
And all the be
For joy our Lo

And all the bells
On earth did ring
A welcome to our
On Christ's Sunday

HEROD *does not sing, and*
entrance until the rest of the p
and grouped themselves – the
lined up to face the audience.

ANGEL (*as soon as*
Behold, I bring y
all people. Glory
goodwill towards

HEROD *now c*

HEROD. Goodwi
believe they ar
good governm

As he comes
from him a
and quietl
audience.

Herod the
west, the R
In the mid
If I lean
Rome: if
to fight P
to choose
Egypt th
am not
Roman
ment o

The
HEF
one

The
Rom
our
bet
ete
ca

ANGEL (*interrupting him in the tone of a palace official*). King Herod. There are three visitors to Jerusalem asking for an audience.

HEROD (*casually*). Where do they come from?

ANGEL. Persia.

HEROD (*in alarm*). Eh? Where is my Secretary?

SECRETARY. Sir?

HEROD. What's this about Persia?

SECRETARY. They are not an official delegation. They said they want a private audience. They would not state their business. One of them is an African. Sir: I think we had better be careful. . . . Do you want to see them?

HEROD. Ah? Yes, I'll see them. But just you stay in the corner and listen to what they say. You may have to send a report to Caesar to keep my name clear. Do you understand?

SECRETARY. Yes. . . .

The WISE MEN *have risen and the* SECRETARY *beckons them forward.*

The king is waiting, gentlemen. Will you come this way?

They present themselves on the stage in front of HEROD. *The* SECRETARY *steps back a pace towards his seat, but does not sit down.*

HEROD. Good morning.

WISE MEN. Your Majesty.

They make a formal bow. HEROD *considers them carefully.*

HEROD. Gentlemen . . from Persia, I believe.

BLACK WISE MAN. The Empire of our Great King encloses more than one land.

HEROD (*a little irritated by this enigmatic answer, but attempting the same tone*). The greatness of a king may be measured less by his lands than by the devotion of his subjects.

YOUNG WISE MAN. Better five men of righteous life than a multitude of evildoers.

BLACK WISE MAN. Evil is more of the mind than of the actions. The slothful man is in many ways found worse than the murderer.

OLD WISE MAN. If we can say that we live, then surely we must die. Who shall number the self-deceivings of the human heart?

The WISE MEN *silently congratulate themselves upon the fluency of their precepts.* HEROD *looks at them sideways.*

HEROD. Deceit is not always plain to see. To be wise, the honest man must often put on an appearance of falsehood. (*He suddenly thrusts a question at the* OLD WISE MAN.) What does the King of Persia want?

OLD WISE MAN (*not disconcerted*). The mind of the Great King is not always penetrable to the thoughts of his subjects, otherwise how should he be called Great?

HEROD (*trying the* BLACK WISE MAN). It is written, is it not, out of Africa comes always something new? You, sir, be so good as to tell me, what is your novelty?

BLACK WISE MAN (*in genuine surprise*). Novelty, your Majesty? But we have come to *you* to find it.

HEROD (*equally surprised, but concealing it*). Indeed. A poor kingdom here: little food, little land, many people, a great deal of danger. I am sorry, my politics are quite without novelty.

BLACK WISE MAN (*knowingly*). Politics and philosophy are not incompatible. Who knows but we discover both in the one revelation?

HEROD (*in annoyance*). Eh, what? Enough of this. I do not understand you.

ANGEL (*quietly*). King Herod, perhaps *they* do not understand *you*.

YOUNG WISE MAN (*complacently*). We understand nothing. All that we do is to read the stars – as some read history books, or as others read geometry.

OLD WISE MAN. The stars have said: 'King Herod.'

YOUNG WISE MAN. 'Jerusalem.'

BLACK WISE MAN. 'The birth of a child.'

HEROD (*bewildered*). Child.

BLACK WISE MAN (*knowingly*). Why not? Great kings have many wives. Many wives have many children. (*Obsequiously*.) Permit us to visit the young prince and his mother.

HEROD (*trying to control the situation*). Visit? . . . What for?

YOUNG WISE MAN. We have been told by the stars that when we see him we shall know.

OLD WISE MAN. Until then, you see, we must be bewildered. Please show us the child.

YOUNG WISE MAN. Please.

WISE MEN. Please, sir, show us the child.

> HEROD *steps aside from them, beckoning the* SECRETARY, *and speaks urgently to him in a whisper:*

HEROD. What are they talking about? Everybody knows I have had no children.

SECRETARY. There must be a mistake.

HEROD. Whose mistake? Mine? What has this to do with Persia? Each of these men dangles from the King of Persia's fingers.

ANGEL. Be careful.

HEROD. I will be careful . . . (*He returns to the* WISE MEN, *his tone now more confident*.) Gentlemen, we are not at one. Your stars have deceived you.

BLACK WISE MAN (*shocked*). That is not possible.

HEROD. Then you have misread them. Study them again. Come back next week. I regret at the moment I have no statement to make.

He and the SECRETARY *return briskly to their seats and sit down. The* WISE MEN *look at each other in some confusion.*

BLACK WISE MAN (*knowingly*). For reasons of state, the king has no statement.

YOUNG WISE MAN (*shakes his head disapprovingly*). Deceit is not always plain. Next week information may be more available.

OLD WISE MAN. He may not have understood.

YOUNG WISE MAN (*sharply*). *We* may not have understood. Gentlemen, we must reconsider our calculations. Politics and philosophy are becoming confused.

BLACK WISE MAN. Yes.

OLD WISE MAN. The interview has been inconclusive. We will repeat it next week.

They return to their places and sit down.

The YOUNG SHEPHERD *rises from his seat, mounts the stage, and walks about blowing on his hands to keep them warm.*

ANGEL. There were shepherds, abiding in the field, keeping watch over their flocks by night.

YOUNG SHEPHERD. Ah, and a cold night – you should say that.

The other two SHEPHERDS *come up on to the stage and sit down on the far side from the pulpit, well downstage, as though they are warming themselves over a fire.*

Have we got a good fire there? We'll want to thaw out a bit after all this.

SOLID SHEPHERD. Are there any of the sheep missing?

YOUNG SHEPHERD. No, I don't think so—I'll have another count.

He goes through the motions of counting sheep.★

Hana mana mona mike
Barcelona bona strike
Hare ware frown venac
Harrico warrico we wo wac
Hana mana mona mike – *etc. . . .*

SOLID SHEPHERD. Comes in any worse than this, we'll be
losing a few of 'em. (*A little noise, off – like a distant cry.*)
Wait up – what's that?

They get to their feet and listen, afraid.

YOUNG SHEPHERD. Sounds like wolves to me. (*To the sheep.*)
Easy, easy now – don't you be feared of it. . . .

SOLID SHEPHERD. Whatever it was, it was over the hill – no
call to be feared of it.

They resume their positions.

OLD SHEPHERD. You certain it was a wolf? Sounded to me
it might be a man making out to be a wolf. There's a lot of
outlandish folk about here these days. I seen 'em on the
roads.

He gets up again uneasily. The SOLID SHEPHERD *reassures
him.*

SOLID SHEPHERD. Coming in for the tax-gathering, that's
all. . . . You registered your name yet?

OLD SHEPHERD. Did it this morning. . . . Tax-gathering or
not, some of 'em could be bandits.

YOUNG SHEPHERD. That's true, you know – they could. I
seen soldiers on the roads. Now why'd there be soldiers if
they hadn't heard word of bandits?

★ This little jargon is a traditional shepherd's counting system
appropriate to the play's original West-Country production. Other
such systems from other parts of England may be found in the *Oxford
Dictionary of Nursery Rhymes* and may be preferred – or if not liked,
may be replaced by ordinary 'one two three', *etc. . .*

OLD SHEPHERD (*doggedly*). Call 'em soldiers, call 'em bandits –
I don't see no difference. You get these soldier-boys up here,
they wouldn't mind taking a beast or two on a dark night.

SOLID SHEPHERD. That's the truth all right, ah, true, true. . . .

The YOUNG SHEPHERD *walks about again, listening.*

YOUNG SHEPHERD. Seems all quiet enough now. . . .

OLD SHEPHERD (*wrapping himself more closely in his blanket*).
Ah. . . .

YOUNG SHEPHERD (*stops walking as a thought troubles him*).
Hey – about this tax-gathering. I've not put my name down
yet.

SOLID SHEPHERD. You'd better do it, son, quick. They'll
be on to you for sure.

YOUNG SHEPHERD (*doubtfully*). I don't like giving up my
name to these fellers.

SOLID SHEPHERD. You'd better do it. They'll run ye in, you
know.

YOUNG SHEPHERD. I thought it was only for householders
and that.

SOLID SHEPHERD (*soberly*). Ah no. You'd better do it.

OLD SHEPHERD. Where were you born?

YOUNG SHEPHERD. Why, Bethlehem, of course – same place
as you – you know that very well.

OLD SHEPHERD. All right, then: you go down to Bethlehem
tomorrow, give in your name, that's all you've got to do.
You do it quick, and they'll leave you alone.

YOUNG SHEPHERD. Ah . . . I don't like giving up my name.
Are they making us pay money?

SOLID SHEPHERD. Not yet they're not.

OLD SHEPHERD. They will. Ha ha. You're not telling me
they'll let us get out of it without paying. I know 'em better
nor that.

They all laugh a little bitterly.

SOLID SHEPHERD. There aren't any of the flock missing, are there?

YOUNG SHEPHERD. No, I just counted.

OLD SHEPHERD. The old one with the broken horn?

YOUNG SHEPHERD. She's there.

SOLID SHEPHERD. We're all right, then.

OLD SHEPHERD. Sit down, lad, keep warm. Here, take a drop o' this.

The YOUNG SHEPHERD *sits down with them and the* OLD SHEPHERD *passes his flask. They each take a drink appreciatively, yawning. The* OLD SHEPHERD *starts to sing, more to himself than at large.*

> I came to town to see my true love
> But I found her gone and far away
> Deluded by an Irish sailor
> Who took her off on a rainy day—

YOUNG SHEPHERD. That's a sad one, isn't it?

OLD SHEPHERD. Ah . . . it's a sad world. Cold enough, anyways. . . . All right, then, we try another: let's warm it up for us.

He sings another song.

> Who'll lend me sixpence?
> All I want is sixpence.

To the SOLID SHEPHERD

Now you.

SOLID SHEPHERD (*singing*).

> To buy a pair of red leather boots
> A wide black hat and a new blue jacket.

OLD SHEPHERD (*to the* YOUNG SHEPHERD). You.

YOUNG SHEPHERD (*singing*).

> If you lend him sixpence
> I swear to you you'll soon regret it.

OLD SHEPHERD. All right, not bad: now we sing her in a round.

They sing the song again as a three-part round, and continue singing it until, one by one, they yawn, stop singing, roll themselves up in their blankets, and fall asleep on the stage – well to one side to allow room for the next action.

The HOSTESS *leaves her place and comes forward with a broom, sweeping busily, talking to the audience as she does so.*

HOSTESS. It's not as if they were all paying for their rooms neither – half of 'em come here with a piece of yellow paper – 'A Government chit, madam, it'll be charged to your credit from the beginning of the next Revenue Period – take it to the Town Hall.' The way my house is at the moment, you'd think *I* was running the Town Hall. Civil Servants . . . Then there's the Military – *they* don't pay neither. 'Haw haw, landlady, I want accommodation for a corporal and thirteen men of Number Eight Detail, three nights altogether, breakfasts and suppers, find their own dinners: but you'll have to provide cooking facilities. . . . Oh yes, and covered storage for the transport. See the place is clean.' Oh, I could lie down and die! To say nothing of the rest of 'em. 'Have you got a room, please?' 'Could you let us have a bed, missus?' 'Just a corner, just a mattress, just a bit of straw – every house in the place is full, we've been all round the town.' I know very well they're full. *I'm* full! No vacancies! Not any more. I mean it. Why should I have my premises made a scapegoat for administrative incompetence and I don't care who hears me!

ANGEL (*sternly*). Madam, be careful. The decree has gone out from Caesar Augustus.

HOSTESS (*shaking her broom at him angrily*). I am perfectly aware of it, young man. That's exactly what I mean. All done as usual with no thought whatever for the convenience of individuals . . . Where was I?

ANGEL. Administrative incompetence.

HOSTESS. Oh there's more to it than that, you know. It's not just incompetence – it's the downright inhumanity that makes me so upset.

As she says this JOSEPH *and* MARY *enter through the stage entrance and come out from behind the pulpit. She half turns and points them out to the audience.*

This poor girl from the north – all that long way in such terrible weather and the baby due any minute. . . . What do they expect me to do? I haven't a room in the house. (*She turns and speaks to* MARY.) What do you expect me to do, dear? I don't know whether I'm on me head or me heels – just look at the place, all chockablock and I'm run off me feet! You'll have to find somewhere else.

She resumes her sweeping, angrily.

JOSEPH (*worried but obstinate*). The fact is, we've tried everywhere.

HOSTESS (*doubtfully*). What about outside the village – there *are* one or two farmhouses where they sometimes take people. I could give you the addresses—

JOSEPH (*considering this pessimistically*). Outside? I don't know about that. It says Bethlehem, you see, black and white, down on the document—(*He shows her an official paper which he takes from his pocket.*) Look. I very much doubt if the authorities would allow . . . (*He looks indecisively from the* HOSTESS *to* MARY.) Besides, I don't know that we dare waste any more time. She ought to be under a roof and that's the plain truth.

HOSTESS (*obviously disturbed*). Oh, yes, I know. I can see. I do understand – oh dear, oh dear . . . (*An idea strikes her, but she hardly likes to suggest it.*) Look, would it be all right if I was to put you in the stable? (*She goes on with a rush in case of objections.*) I mean, just for tonight, till we can get a bit of space organized. It won't be too bad in there; there's plenty of straw and that, and we can keep the animals separate – I could give it a clean-out first.

JOSEPH (*much relieved*). We're not ones to grumble, ma'am; anything at all, you know – we'd be very very grateful – oh no, we're not choosey—

HOSTESS (*embarrassed*). Yes, yes, well – over here, you come along, my dear, you take my arm, that's right – (*She takes* MARY *by the arm and leads her upstage to the central rostrum.* JOSEPH *makes to follow, but she firmly prevents him.*) Oh no – you stay here. (*She settles* MARY *down on the rostrum, which need only be raised a few inches from the main stage level.*)

> JOSEPH, *after a moment of indecision, comes downstage and sings, quietly, towards the audience, from underneath the pulpit.*

JOSEPH (*singing*).

> Joseph was an old man
> And an old man was he
> When he married Mary
> In the land of Galilee.

> *The* HOSTESS *suddenly stands up and comes down from the rostrum, looking about her anxiously.*

HOSTESS. I'd better get the midwife – where's the midwife?

> *The* MIDWIFE *stands up in her place.*

MIDWIFE. Do you want me, dear?

> *She comes downstage. The* HOSTESS *takes her by the arm.*

HOSTESS. Yes, quick, come to the stable!

MIDWIFE (*shocked*). The stable!

HOSTESS (*embarrassed*). It's the best I could do. . . . *She leads the* MIDWIFE *up to* MARY.

JOSEPH (*singing*).

> As Joseph was a-walking
> He heard an angel sing
> This night shall be born
> Our heavenly king.

MARY, *seated on the rostrum with the* HOSTESS *and the* MIDWIFE *bending over her at each side, speaks to the audience.*

MARY.

Nine months we sit and wait and dream.
Quiet in dreams and quiet in fear.

ANGEL (*to audience*).

Young wives of honest men:
The time is near.
Your work is made
That will be yours no longer.
Say good-bye. Let go.

MARY.

What we have made
We learn to leave alone.
What we now know
From now must live unknown.

She folds her hands across her belly.

Good-bye, good-bye.
I have come to let you go.

She bows herself down on the rostrum.

JOSEPH (*singing*).

> He neither shall be born
> In housen nor in hall
> Nor in the place of Paradise
> But in an ox's stall.

He neither shall be clothed
In purple nor in pall
But all in fair linen
As were babies all.

He neither shall be rocked
In silver nor in gold
But in a wooden cradle
That rocks on the mould.

The HOSTESS *and the* MIDWIFE *have moved aside and are waiting, looking towards* MARY, *who kneels alone with her back to the Audience. When* JOSEPH *has finished singing he sits down at the base of the pulpit, on the small step that should be provided there.*

The ANGEL *leans out of the pulpit and suddenly shouts across the stage at the sleeping* SHEPHERDS *in a vigorous urgent voice:*

ANGEL. Who's awake! Hey-ey, shepherds, up up, who's awake!

They wake, startled and confused. The YOUNG SHEPHERD *staggers to his feet.*

YOUNG SHEPHERD (*dazed*). Eh, what, what is it?
ANGEL. Wake up, wake up!
YOUNG SHEPHERD. What's the matter? Where are the sheep?

He wanders vaguely about, looking for them. The other SHEPHERDS *also pull themselves to their feet. Throughout this passage they must not appear to see the* ANGEL.

ANGEL. Safe and sound. All safe where you put them.
YOUNG SHEPHERD. Who are you? I can't see you. Who is it calling?
SOLID SHEPHERD. Who is it?
OLD SHEPHERD. What's the matter – where are the sheep – wolves – bandits. . .?

The SHEPHERDS *move about in confusion, getting in each other's way. The* ANGEL *now speaks to them in a quieter but no less urgent voice.*

ANGEL. Fear not.
SOLID SHEPHERD (*restraining the other two*). Wait. Listen!

The SHEPHERDS *stand still. They listen, but do not look directly up at the* ANGEL.

ANGEL. Fear not. For behold, I bring you good tidings of great joy, which shall be to all people. For unto you is born this day in the City of David a Saviour, which is Christ the Lord. And this shall be a sign unto you; ye shall find the babe wrapped in swaddling clothes, lying in a manger.

The SHEPHERDS *cluster together, astonished.*

SOLID SHEPHERD. Here, I don't like this –
YOUNG SHEPHERD. Did you hear what it said?
SOLID SHEPHERD. Somebody's having a game with us. They're trying to make us fools—
OLD SHEPHERD (*doubtfully*). Why don't we go to the town and see?
SOLID SHEPHERD. See?
YOUNG SHEPHERD. Why don't we go there?
SOLID SHEPHERD. What do you mean, go there?
YOUNG SHEPHERD. Down to the town.
OLD SHEPHERD (*regretting his impulse*). No. No. I don't think I like to.
ANGEL. Glory to God in the Highest, and on earth peace: good will towards men.
YOUNG SHEPHERD. Come on, I'm going –

The ANGEL *now continues to repeat his last line, which – if convenient to the production – may be picked up and augmented by voices from different places round the building*

out of sight of the audience. This repetition of the 'Glory'
continues in crescendo throughout the ensuing dialogue. The
YOUNG SHEPHERD *tugs vainly at the sleeve of the* SOLID
SHEPHERD.

Come *on*!

Giving up the SOLID SHEPHERD *as a bad job, he leaves him,*
jumps down from the stage, and sets off rapidly round the
hall to the back of the audience.

OLD SHEPHERD. Wait, hey, wait for me—

He comes down from the stage and hobbles after the YOUNG
SHEPHERD. *The* SOLID SHEPHERD *remains alone in an*
agony of indecision.

SOLID SHEPHERD. Why don't they leave us alone! We were
doing a job of work, that's all – you've got no right to
meddle with the lives of working men! (*He calls after his*
colleagues.) Hey, wait, wait for me – wait—

He, too, jumps from the stage and runs after the others.
When they reach the rear of the hall they wait there quietly
for their next cue. The ANGEL'S *'Glory' now comes to an*
end.

MARY *stands up and turns to face the audience. She is*
holding a baby in her arms. She starts to walk downstage,
the HOSTESS *and the* MIDWIFE *coming with her on either*
side. JOSEPH *rises and helps her to sit down on a stool, which*
he can fetch unobtrusively from behind the pulpit.

JOSEPH.

> He came all so still
> Where His mother was
> As dew in April
> That falleth on the grass.

He came all so still
To his mother's bower
As dew in April
That falleth on the flower.

As he speaks this verse, the SHEPHERDS *slowly advance through the audience. They stop at the foot of the stage steps.*

SOLID SHEPHERD. Why, it *is* a baby.
YOUNG SHEPHERD. That's right.
SOLID SHEPHERD. A little boy?

They climb up on to the stage.

We didn't dream it.
YOUNG SHEPHERD. No.
OLD SHEPHERD. Can we have a look at him, missus?
MIDWIFE (*bossily*). Now be very careful, don't breathe too near him. Quietly, young man, quietly, don't make such a disturbance with your great big boots now – *careful!*
HOSTESS (*fussing about*). Now you're not to upset the poor young lady, she's very very tired. If you don't want them in, dear, you just say so to me, and I'll send them straight out.
MARY (*listlessly*). No, they can come.

They come nearer with clumsy consideration and bend to see the baby.

OLD SHEPHERD (*holding out his hand*). Hey, you hold my finger, boy – can you do that? Clutch it? Ah, that's the feller – he knows how to make an effort, don't he now? You look at him – strong! He likes me! Now you go to sleep now, and let your mam have a bit of rest . . . mind if I sing to him, eh?

He sings, quietly.

Go to sleep, little baby, and then you will see
How strong grows the acorn on the branches of the tree.
B.G.G.–C

How tightly it lives in the green and the brown
But the strong storms of autumn will soon shake it down.

The deeper it falls then the stronger will it tower
Bold roots and wide limbs and a true heart of power.

Though the oak is the master of all the trees on the hill
His heart will be mastered by the carpenter's will.

SOLID SHEPHERD. Build a roof for your house, boy, the oak
tree will – keel and planks for your boat if you want to
go a voyage, cradle for you to sleep in – you grow up as
strong as that – oh you'll be the rare master!

YOUNG SHEPHERD. Hey, missus, do you know, we heard
this in a dream? We all dreamed it, you see, all three of
us. . . . 'In the City of David, a Saviour which is Christ
the Lord. And lying in a manger.'

OLD SHEPHERD. That's right. It said that.

SOLID SHEPHERD. We don't know what to think, missus. Do
you think it could be true?

MARY.

Nine months ago I dreamed a dream:
A white fish swam into my heart.
I took my hand and pulled it out:
But the hands of the strong men tore the little fish apart.

JOSEPH. Believe it to be true and celebrate it. All these things
will be known, in good time. Here is the baby: here is his
mother . . . your sheep are left out on the hills. You had
better go back now and look after them. If it was a good
dream: then you will dream it again one day. If it wasn't –
well, the world has to carry on turning. There are trees
must be cut down and the timber to be shaped, there are
houses to need roofs, the ships to need their frames, there
are always the cradles will need to be rocked. And each one
of these works will call for its true attention . . . Thank you
for coming.

MARY. Thank you.

MIDWIFE (*bossy again*). Now I think that's enough, I'm sure you've had enough, dear – (*She feels* MARY'S *brow*.) Yes, we're getting rather tired – you'd better go now, quietly, quietly, thank you very much – it's very important at this stage, lots of rest and quiet – *thank* you.

THE SHEPHERDS. God give you good health and strengthen the child.

> *They withdraw quietly, and take their original places in front of the pulpit, below the stage. As soon as they are gone, the* MIDWIFE *and* HOSTESS *gather in on* MARY. *The* HOSTESS *picks up the baby.*

HOSTESS. You'd better let me take him now, dear.

MIDWIFE (*sharply*). Not too long for the first time.

HOSTESS (*to* MARY). We've got to conserve our energies, haven't we? (*Sharply, to* MIDWIFE.) *I* know, dear – I've had four of 'em myself. . . . There, there, the little lamb, there, the little precious – oh he's a lovely boy, dear, he's going to make you so happy – don't you carry on now, about all those rough fellows trampling in. I think they'd all had a drop too much, if you ask me—

> *The* MIDWIFE *butts in again, pulling the* HOSTESS *by the elbow.*

MIDWIFE. She ought to be moved, you know. We can't have her lying in a stable *now*.

HOSTESS (*worried again all of a sudden*). But I haven't a room in the house.

MIDWIFE (*decisively*). Then she'd better come to my place. . . . You'll come to my place, dear, won't you? You can have my bed, you see, and I can sleep in the kitchen.

JOSEPH (*worrying*). But we couldn't put you out like that—

MARY. Thank you, you are very kind.

HOSTESS (*glad to be rid of the responsibility*). Don't talk, dear, don't exhaust yourself—

MIDWIFE. That's right, there we are—

> *The* HOSTESS *and the* MIDWIFE *help* MARY *away and install her on a seat beside the* MIDWIFE'S. JOSEPH *follows and stands beside his wife – they are partly concealed by the pulpit and remain out of the action for a while. The* HOSTESS *and the* MIDWIFE *resume their seats.* HEROD *rises and comes forward.*

HEROD. Those three from Persia – they should be here today. Where are they?

SECRETARY (*rising and coming up to him*). They are waiting to see you, sir. Shall I bring them in?

HEROD. If you would be so good.

> HEROD *takes his stance downstage, confidently. The* SECRETARY *beckons to the* WISE MEN, *who rise and come to the king.*

Gentlemen, good morning.

WISE MEN. Good morning, Your Majesty.

> *They bow, formally.*

HEROD (*genially*). I owe you an apology. On your previous visit, I was unaccountably obtuse. Although the blame must to some extent lie with my advisers. I had not been supplied with the necessary information. Had I?

SECRETARY (*playing the comedy*). No, sir, you had not. Gentlemen, may I, too, apologize for the inadequacies of his Majesty's staff. We entirely regret the misunderstanding.

> *The* WISE MEN *bow politely.*

HEROD. When you spoke of a prince, I naturally concluded you were referring to a member of my own household. Alas, Heaven has graced me with no recent issue.

WISE MEN(*formally*). Alas.

HEROD (*echoing their manner*). Gentlemen, alas . . . But—
(*He looks keenly at them and adopts a sharper tone.*) But to
ascertain the truth from the stars, it is necessary to remem-
ber the recurrent cloudiness of the firmament. As no doubt
you have realized.

OLD WISE MAN (*waiting for what is coming*). In science, even
yet, there is no complete certainty.

HEROD. Nor is the possibility of human error ever to be
underrated. As no doubt you have realized.

BLACK WISE MAN (*slyly*). Yet it is written: even in the depth
of dark winter, the sun may sometimes be descried shining
with unlooked-for brilliance.

YOUNG WISE MAN (*sardonic*). It is also written that the
flowers brought forth to greet such winter sun are likely to
fade and die in the frost of the evening.

OLD WISE MAN (*checking his colleague with a slight gesture*).
This is perhaps beside the point: for, Your Majesty, *we* have
yet to see any sign of the sun at all.

HEROD (*enjoying himself*). Aha, is that so? Wise men from
the east? There are wise men in Jerusalem. I have been
asking them some questions since our last meeting. . . .
(*He has turned his back casually: now he whips round to startle
them.*) Gentlemen: Bethlehem!

WISE MEN(*surprised*). Bethlehem?

> HEROD *takes an impressive scroll which the* SECRETARY *is
> holding in readiness for him.*

HEROD (*reading with emphasis*). 'And thou, Bethlehem, in the
land of Judah, art not least among the cities of Judah, for
out of thee shall come a Governor that shall rule my people
Israel.' . . . A history lesson, gentlemen. (*He finds a
different place in the scroll, as pointed out by the* SECRETARY,
and reads further.) 'Abraham begat Isaac, and Isaac begat
Jacob, and Jacob begat Judah – and his brethren – and

Judah begat Phares, and Phares begat . . .' (*He skips a bit.*)
. . . 'Begat – one, two, three – seven generations: and the
seventh was Obed, and Obed begat Jesse, and Jesse begat
David the King!' (*He looks at them significantly over the
scroll.*) Now David the King was begotten in Bethlehem,
and I must confess to you, gentlemen, that I myself am not
among his posterity. So, therefore, any prince liable to find
loyalty in Israel, who does not spring from Herod, will in all
probability spring from the seed of David; and according to
the logic of prophecy – which I am sure you will understand
– you must look for him in Bethlehem. Jerusalem is no
good. I am sorry to have wasted your time.

The WISE MEN *are somewhat disconcerted.*

OLD WISE MAN. Your Majesty, will you excuse me while I
confer with my colleagues?

HEROD *nods graciously, and the three of them get into a
huddle and whisper rapidly together.*

YOUNG WISE MAN. Your Majesty, would you permit us to
study the documents?

HEROD, *enjoying himself, hands the scroll to the* SECRE-
TARY, *who gives it to the* YOUNG WISE MAN. *They return
to their huddle and study it. While they do so* HEROD
addresses them genially.

HEROD. The information is taken from the prophetic books of
Israel. I can assure you it has been collated for me under
conditions of the most exhaustive scholarship.

THE WISE MEN *come to a unanimous decision, and turn
to face the king.*

OLD WISE MAN. Your Majesty, we will go to Bethlehem. This
could be an occasion of the utmost importance.

HEROD (*pleasantly*). You will inform me directly, whatever you find ?

OLD WISE MAN. Your Majesty, without fail.

They are about to bow and make their farewell. HEROD *interrupts them, casually.*

HEROD. One further point. The stars. How long have you been observing this new revelation ?

BLACK WISE MAN. It has been visible for two years. It took us a year to calculate the significance, and then the preparations for the journey, the travelling itself, the—

HEROD (*cutting him short*). Thank you, gentlemen. I understand. Good morning. I look forward to your news.

Before they quite realize it, the audience is over, HEROD *and the* SECRETARY *have returned to their seats, and they are left alone on the forestage.* HEROD *and the* SECRETARY *do not sit down, but stand there with their backs turned.*

WISE MEN (*a little put out by this abruptness*). Thank you, Your Majesty. Good morning. . . .

They bow towards the place where he stood, and then leave the stage and walk in a stately manner up the hall to the rear of the audience.

HEROD *walks back across the stage, and the* SECRETARY *sits down.* HEROD *looks up and catches the* ANGEL'S *eye.*

HEROD (*irritably*). It was necessary to tell them. If I had pretended I had heard nothing about any prophecies, they would have found out I was lying, and in the end they would still have gone to Bethlehem. The difference would have been they would never have come back to tell me what they found. . . . (*He is troubled in his mind.*) Supposing a Son of David *should* have been born: and supposing he is demonstrated to carry some Divine Marks of Royalty – or whatever the book says ?

ANGEL (*deadpan*). The situation should be within your control. Are you not the king?

HEROD (*petulantly*). I am not trained to understand prophecies and superstitions! Those that do understand them have assured me that it is very unwise to ignore their political importance. Here are the King of Persia's men, looking for what might well be a claimant to the ancient line of Israel. If Persia determines to recognize such a claimant, Rome will punish *me*.

ANGEL. How?

HEROD. How do you imagine? They will send in an army to secure their Legitimate Interests. A Roman Governor will be appointed in Jerusalem. If I am lucky, I may be permitted to wash up in his kitchen.

ANGEL. And if not?

HEROD (*making a despairing gesture*). Ah. . . . Wheresoever the carcass is, there will the Eagles be gathered together.

ANGEL. Surely your loyalty to Caesar will not so easily be doubted?

HEROD (*bitterly*). My loyalty to Caesar is continually being doubted – and not without some reason. . . . (*He speaks now with great sincerity.*) I am not primarily concerned with my own personal fortunes. The object of my life is the integrity of my kingdom. What am I to do?

ANGEL. You had better wait and see what the three gentlemen discover.

HEROD. (*He suddenly looks up sharply, puzzled*). Who *are* you?

> The ANGEL *shrugs unhelpfully.*
> HEROD *glares up at him with defiance.*

Do you want to see Jerusalem with not one stone left upon another, and in the Temple which *I* built, the Abomination of Desolation standing where it ought not?

ANGEL (*firmly and simply*). No.

HEROD. Then pity the king: and pray for his policy.

He turns sadly away and sits down in his place.

ANGEL (*addressing the audience with sadness*). Not one stone shall be left upon another. . . . Ye shall hear of wars and rumours of wars. And nation shall rise against nation, and kingdom against kingdom: and there shall be famines and pestilences and earthquakes in divers places. (*His voice rises in a torrent.*) And there shall be signs in the sun and in the moon and in the stars, and upon the earth distress of nations, with perplexity; the sea and the waves roaring; men's hearts failing them for fear and for looking after those things which are coming on the earth: for the powers of heaven shall be shaken! (*He seems for a moment afraid of his own vision: then his voice quietens and he delivers his next lines with sober stillness.*) And then they shall see the Son of Man coming in a cloud with power and great glory. Verily I say unto you: this generation shall not pass away till all be fulfilled.

After his words there is a silence, broken by the WISE MEN *approaching the stage through the audience.*

YOUNG WISE MAN (*mounting the stage*). Bethlehem.

The other two join him, and they look around them.

BLACK WISE MAN. I think this is a place that should answer the description.

OLD WISE MAN. Possibly.

BLACK WISE MAN. A small town or large village, agricultural population, one principal hostelry, decidedly third-class— (*He frowns doubtfully.*) Gentlemen, is it likely, do you think, that the king's information can be correct?

OLD WISE MAN. Possibly.

BLACK WISE MAN. Possibly? Oh yes, yes, possible. But I said, is it *likely*? I confess I have my doubts.

YOUNG WISE MAN. You are of the opinion that the king has deceived us?

BLACK WISE MAN. No . . . no . . . I hardly mean quite that.

OLD WISE MAN. The king impressed me as very definitely a man of high intelligence, genuinely understanding the responsibilities of power and with an enlightened attitude towards philosophy and science. I cannot believe that he would wish to deceive us.

BLACK WISE MAN. We could have been mistaken. Are we not all fallible ?

YOUNG WISE MAN (*firmly*). The stars are not fallible. (*He looks up at them, and is suddenly transfixed with excitement.*) Look! Look at the Great Bear – and then look at Orion!

They follow his gaze and are infected with his excitement.

OLD WISE MAN. The Dog Star has retreated!

YOUNG WISE MAN. Yes, but consider the passage of the Moon!

BLACK WISE MAN. Let me see the chart.

The OLD WISE MAN *fumbles in his satchel and produces a rolled-up chart, which he clumsily unfurls.*

YOUNG WISE MAN (*assisting him hastily*). Calculating forward from her last presence in Scorpio—

BLACK WISE MAN (*thrusting between them and snatching the chart*). Let me see the chart!

They all three crowd round it, getting in each other's way.

OLD WISE MAN. Why should we find the Dog Star diminished, yet Mars is still flamboyant ?

BLACK WISE MAN (*decisively*). Look, gentlemen: look at the chart, and look again at the Heavens! The king has *not* deceived us. *We* have been blind. It *is* here, in Bethlehem, that our treasure will be found. Let us go forward, and see!

The MIDWIFE *rises and comes forward hesitantly.*

MIDWIFE. Who are these gentlemen?

ANGEL. They have come from a far country. They are here to see the baby.

MIDWIFE (*nervously*). Political gentlemen?

ANGEL. No, not exactly. Scientific and philosophical. Very wise, very important. . . . So, sirs, you have arrived. What do you expect to find?

The WISE MEN *draw themselves up authoritatively, but have no very clear answer.*

BLACK WISE MAN. We – we have brought gifts.

YOUNG WISE MAN. We are certain, without doubt, that a new age may well be at hand.

OLD WISE MAN. We must be ready to welcome it. We must not be left behind.

BLACK WISE MAN. Gifts, we have brought. We chose them symbolically. . . . Madam, if you please: may we see the Child?

If the cast allows of the WISE MEN *having* ATTENDANTS, *the* OLD WISE MAN *at this point signals towards the rear of the hall and the three* ATTENDANTS *come through the audience, each carrying his master's gift. These gifts should be elaborate caskets of some size. If the* WISE MEN *have to carry their own gifts, they can be smaller, and can be carried in satchels. In such case the satchels should appear to be made of rich materials – not any old bags.*

The MIDWIFE *now turns and beckons forward* MARY, *who comes, carrying the baby.* JOSEPH *is behind her, and assists her to sit down on the same stool as she used to greet the* SHEPHERDS. *The* WISE MEN *seem a little unsure of themselves and give the impression of having expected something very different.*

OLD WISE MAN (*looking vaguely from* MIDWIFE *to* MARY). The mother? Which is she? Is the mother not here?

BLACK WISE MAN (*addressing* MARY, *once she has sat down*). Dear lady, our congratulations. (*They bow to her politely. The* ATTENDANTS (*if any*) *have ranged themselves on the stage, kneeling, and holding up their gifts.*) For the child, we have brought gifts.

> *Each* WISE MAN *in turn takes his gift from the* ATTENDANT *and holds it up to the audience, describing it; and then turns and presents it to* MARY – *or rather, holds it up to her and then lays it on the stage at her feet.*

Gold. Gold speaks of power. Where there is power there lie the benefits for the future generations.

YOUNG WISE MAN. Frankincense. Frankincense speaks of religion. As men of science, we cannot but recognize those great forces in our lives we do not fully understand.

OLD WISE MAN. Myrrh. Myrrh speaks of death, and no one can escape it. Yet in a well-governed land the good work of one man will be continued by his successors. (*A slight pause. The* WISE MEN *look at one another, and at* MARY *with the baby. The* OLD WISE MAN *clears his throat and offers a general sentiment on behalf of the others.*) We are confident that this Son of David, to whom we bring our gifts, will prove a notable descendant of his most notable forefathers: it is, in fact, so written in the ordering of the constellations. Hence our visit – we thank you—

> *He glances at his colleagues, and they pick up their cue.*

WISE MEN. We thank you for permitting us to welcome your son. You have given us an experience of the utmost importance.

MARY. Thank you.

> *The* WISE MEN *bow and withdraw a little.*

WISE MEN. Good day, dear lady. Thank you.

They bow again. MARY *and* JOSEPH *withdraw, the* MID-WIFE *follows, carrying the gifts. The* WISE MEN *turn their backs upon them, and confer, facing the audience.*

BLACK WISE MAN. Well.

OLD WISE MAN. Well?

YOUNG WISE MAN. I do not understand it.

OLD WISE MAN. Of course, it *is* the Son of David, the stars have made it clear, the mother did not deny it. But the significance? Why, I had expected—

BLACK WISE MAN. I too had expected . . . These people obviously have nothing to do with politics. And I see no connexion either with religion or with prophecies, or with anything else. Except that—

YOUNG WISE MAN. Except that we were *told*. Except that *we* were told. And *what* have we been told?

BLACK WISE MAN. No, I do not know. . . . And even if this *is* a true Prince of Israel—

ANGEL (*he offers his remarks like a prompter, and the* WISE MEN *accept them into their conversation without realizing who is speaking*). Even if this *is* a true Prince of Israel?

YOUNG WISE MAN (*thoughtfully*). It will do him little good for us to declare it.

OLD WISE MAN (*sharply*). Herod?

ANGEL. Herod. Yes, Herod.

BLACK WISE MAN (*quickly*). Do you think—

OLD WISE MAN. I think—

ANGEL. I think you would be best advised—

YOUNG WISE MAN. I think we would be best advised to leave the country quietly and forget the whole business.

BLACK WISE MAN. Yes, very true: I think that *is* wisest.

ANGEL. You had better go home.

OLD WISE MAN (*hurrying down from the stage*). We had better go home!

The other two follow him and they hasten one after the other through the audience towards the rear of the hall.

BLACK WISE MAN. Yes. Quickly. Now!

YOUNG WISE MAN. Don't look behind you! We might be being followed!

OLD WISE MAN. Quick, quickly, home, we have got to get home!

They run out of the hall without stopping – if there are ATTENDANTS, *these follow them in equal panic. The door slams, and their shouts and footsteps die away outside. There is a moment of quiet as the* ANGEL *looks keenly towards the door; then, without turning his head, he beckons to* JOSEPH.

ANGEL. Joseph, come here. (JOSEPH *comes forward and stands by the pulpit in some surprise.*) Are you afraid of the great men of the world?

JOSEPH. No, sir, I am not. I am a carpenter and a good craftsman. I stand firm by my trade – good joints in good timber.

ANGEL. You have married a dangerous wife.

JOSEPH (*stubbornly*). I married who it was my concern to marry. I do not know why you should be commenting upon it.

ANGEL. There are thousands of carpenters in the provinces of Egypt. Too many for anyone to ask what sort of wives they have, there.

JOSEPH (*thinking hard*). Or what sort of children. . . . The question about danger. How close?

ANGEL. Tonight.

JOSEPH (*in consternation*). Tonight?

ANGEL. She is well enough to travel?

JOSEPH. I think so—

ANGEL. Very well then. Go!

MARY *has come quietly forward and catches the last few words of this dialogue.*

MARY (*to the* ANGEL). I can see that you have made my husband afraid. He is not a timorous man. What have you told him ? What is to happen ? Who are they going to kill ?

ANGEL.

The King, if they can.

The axe will drive into the timber

And the leaves are not yet green.

JOSEPH.

What are you talking about – King ?

King Herod, do you mean ?

ANGEL.

Green leaves for that one ?

No, sir, he is red and he is gold

And he will fall. On which day

And in which year has not yet been foretold.

But there is to be time for the next King to grow,

Short time, narrow time, time enough to know

That the night will be over

And the day will be wide

And as wide as the world.

MARY.

Let the waters be beaten so yet the ship will sail,

Let the wind be driven, but the house yet hold its roof,

Let the timbers only be seasoned under the strong dry sun.

ANGEL (*disturbed*).

So that they may hang, and creak,

And grind, and bear against the strain ?

Run to Egypt in the dark

And then come slowly home.

> *They turn away from the* ANGEL *and walk about the stage for a turn or two. The* FARM-GIRL *comes from her place towards the front of the stage. She walks up and down, going through the motions of sowing corn from a sack, and singing as she does so.* MARY *and* JOSEPH *stop, as though to rest by the roadside, further upstage.*

FARM-GIRL (*sings*).

> The seed is set into the ground
> At the darkening of the year,
> When the rain runs down in the cold kirk town
> And the roofs are hung with fear.
>
> The grain is scattered on the land
> At the side of Egypt's road.
> God send the proud young harvesters
> A full and golden load.

She looks up and sees JOSEPH *and* MARY.

You seem to be lost. Can I show you the way?

JOSEPH. We were on the road to Egypt, but I don't know whether we are going right – can you tell us, please?

FARM-GIRL (*looking hard at them*). Surely, why not? You go straight ahead, you see, keeping to the west and the south, you cross over that river, and there you are in Egypt.

JOSEPH. Thank you. . . . I wonder – if anyone comes after us – I mean – anyone to be afraid of – you won't tell them you've seen us?

FARM-GIRL (*suddenly hostile*). Afraid of? You mean soldiers? You mean you're in trouble? Look, my father's farm stands right by the frontier. We have to take care what we say to soldiers. If they ask me the truth, I daren't tell 'em any other. How do I know you've not been sent to spy, so they can burn down our house? Go on, go to Egypt – if they ask me anything I shall have to tell 'em true!

MARY. Joseph, this way, she said west and then south, quick, quick, hurry to the river. . . .

She and JOSEPH *hasten out by the stage door.*

FARM-GIRL (*appealing to the audience*). They burn houses. I've seen them. Kill my husband, kill the children, take all the last harvest stored in the barns. What about my father?

He's been ill in bed all the winter. They say there's not a farm on the frontier lasts more than twenty years. I've seen some burnt three times in two years. We have to take care.

> HEROD *and the* SECRETARY *come from their places and the* FARM-GIRL *retreats in alarm to the base of the pulpit.*

HEROD. Straight away from Bethlehem—

SECRETARY. By the least-frequented road—

HEROD. Without one word to me!

SECRETARY. They are over the frontier and back half-way to Persia.

HEROD. What did they find?

SECRETARY. Not necessarily anything.

HEROD. Not necessarily? Of course they did. Rabbit holes under my walls.

SECRETARY. Rabbit holes?

HEROD. Yes. Burrowing in. Scrabbling. Put traps in the holes . . . Inform my officers I want a complete investigation. The unity of this kingdom has been thrust into peril— (*The* SECRETARY *goes and sits down:* HEROD *shakes his arm at the* ANGEL.)

Don't you tell me to be careful! I *am* being careful!

ANGEL. Careful: and afraid.

HEROD. Of course I am afraid.

ANGEL. Tell me what of.

HEROD. The end of my world. The end of peace of life. The end of good order. . . . The king must rule his human subjects by means of his own humanity. And naturally, within his rule must be comprehended such difficult extremes of good and of evil as may be found from one end to the other of his unfortunate kingdom. . . . (*He assumes a rhetorical posture, and addresses the audience.*) Citizens! Patriots! Through the years I have been your leader I have kept you free from war and provided unexampled prosperity. You are richer and happier than ever you have been! Your

children are receiving opportunities for education and
advancement that your own fathers could not have imagined
in their wildest dreams. Dare you see this prosperity de-
stroyed in one night? You answer me – no. You answer
me – King Herod, do what you believe to be necessary and
we your faithful people will follow you as always in loyalty
and trust! (*To the* ANGEL.) You understand – I am putting
a very particular mark against my name in the history books,
and I know it, and I am not afraid. It is fitting that the
honour of one man should die for the good of the people.
(*He beckons to the* SECRETARY, *who rises in his place and
takes a step forward.*) Send out an instruction to my officers.
They are to put to death all the children that are in Bethlehem and in all the coasts thereof from two years old and
under, according to the time which I diligently inquired of
the Wise Men. It is the only safe way. See that it is done.
(*The* SECRETARY *bows and remains standing with lowered
head. To the* ANGEL.) I suppose you will tell me that even
this in some way fulfils some sort of prophecy.

ANGEL. Yes. The Prophet Jeremiah, chapter 31, verse 15. Do
you want to hear it?

HEROD. I have not got time. (*To the* SECRETARY.) Have you
done what I told you?

SECRETARY. Sir, it has been done. Your officers have received
the orders, and are carrying them out.

> *The Massacre is indicated by a sudden clash of cymbals, and
> a loud wailing cry which should proceed from different
> places all around the hall. The actors still on the stage can
> take part in it. This cry dies away as suddenly as it has arisen.*

ANGEL. From the Prophet Jeremiah, chapter 31, verse 15:
'In Rama was there a voice heard – lamentation and weeping
and great mourning. Rachel weeping for her children and
would not be comforted, because they were not.'

HEROD. Very well. I can carry it. All upon one man's back. . . .
   Is it finished?

SECRETARY. Sir, it is finished.

   HEROD *is about to return to his seat.*

ANGEL (*in the voice of a palace official*). One moment. King
   Herod – a message for my lord the king. From the captain
   in command of the road leading south from the city of
   Bethlehem. A man and a woman carrying a young child were
   seen to pass on this road half an hour before your orders
   were received. A patrol has been sent after them: but they
   have not yet been caught.

HEROD. They have gone towards Egypt. They must be held
   before they get there. I know the road to Egypt. There
   are too many secret ways for them to slip across the frontier
   – for instance, this farm. Who does it belong to!

   The FARM-GIRL *comes forward, terrified.*

FARM-GIRL. Lord, this is my father's farm. My husband
   works it for him and I help him to do it. How can we serve
   you, lord?

HEROD. A man and a woman, carrying a young child. Did they
   pass? Did you see them?

FARM-GIRL. Yes, lord, I saw them.

HEROD. When?

FARM-GIRL. Not long since – I'm not certain—

HEROD. *When?*

FARM-GIRL. I was sowing that field; it can't have been more
   than—

HEROD. This field?

FARM-GIRL. Yes, lord—

HEROD. Are you certain of that?

FARM-GIRL. Why, yes, lord, I swear it – I told them I
   couldn't hide them. I always respected the law. I never told
   a lie to the soldiers, not in all my life—

HEROD (*cutting her short in disgust*). This corn has been growing for a couple of months. If anyone crossed here, it's nobody to interest *me*. Hold your noise, woman: you won't suffer any harm. But just you be certain that you and your family always behave. It's not very safe to do anything else.

FARM-GIRL. No, lord, I know. Thank you, lord, thank you. . . .

> *She shrinks again to one side.* HEROD *takes no more notice of her.*

HEROD. I think I have missed them. We followed the wrong road. If it was them at all. I do not know. Nobody knows. I hope it is finished. All of you here; pray for the king and pray this may be finished.

> *He returns to his seat. The* FARM-GIRL *timidly comes forward again.*

FARM-GIRL. That corn grew in one hour. It *was* the right field. How could I tell lies to *him*? Soldiers – he's worse than soldiers – he was the *King*! . . . Oh my Lord God, it grew in one hour. (*She bends down as if examining blades of corn.*) It – it seems to be ordinary corn . . . if we cut it and threshed it and ground it into flour – I don't know that we dare. I don't know how anyone dare eat this piece of bread, without they know first who it was went across it – and who it was, was carried. . . .

> *She retires to her place and sits down.*

ANGEL. And the Prophecy continues. From the Book of the prophet Jeremiah, chapter 31, reading from the sixteenth verse: 'Thus saith the Lord: 'Refrain thy voice from weeping and thine eyes from tears. For thy work shall be rewarded, saith the Lord, and they shall come again from the land of the enemy.' (*The cast on the stage now stand, and line up along the stage front. They are joined by the* WISE MEN *through the stage door.*) 'And there is hope in thine end, saith the Lord. Thy children shall come again, and dwell in their own border.'

The actors on the stage now conclude the play by singing the Corpus Christi Carol.

Down in yon forest there stands a hall:
The bells of Paradise I heard them ring.
It's covered all over with purple and pall:
And I love my Lord Jesus above anything.

In that hall there stands a bed:
The bells of Paradise I heard them ring.
It's covered all over with scarlet so red:
And I love my Lord Jesus above anything.

At the bedside there lies a stone:
The bells of Paradise I heard them ring.
Which the sweet Virgin Mary knelt upon:
And I love my Lord Jesus above anything.

Under that bed there runs a flood:
The bells of Paradise I heard them ring.
The one half runs water, the other half blood:
And I love my Lord Jesus above anything.

At the foot of the bed there grows a thorn:
The bells of Paradise I heard them ring.
Which ever blows blossom since he was born:
And I love my Lord Jesus above anything.

Over the bed the moon shines bright:
The bells of Paradise I heard them ring.
Denoting our Saviour was born this night:
And I love my Lord Jesus above anything.

While they are singing MARY *and* JOSEPH *with the* BABY *come in by the stage door and take their places behind – then the cast opens to let them through, and they lead the procession out of the hall, the* ANGEL *bringing up the rear. The carol should be timed so that all the actors are clear of the hall before they stop singing.*

Methuen's Modern Plays
EDITED BY JOHN CULLEN

Methuen's Theatre Classics

THE REDEMPTION	Adapted by Gordon Honeycombe from five cycles of Mystery Plays
IRONHAND	Goethe adapted by John Arden
BRAND	Ibsen
THE WILD DUCK	translated by
HEDDA GABLER	Michael Meyer
THE MASTER BUILDER	
MISS JULIE	Strindberg translated by Michael Meyer
LADY WINDERMERE'S FAN	Wilde
THE IMPORTANCE OF BEING EARNEST	
THE PLAYBOY OF THE WESTERN WORLD	Synge

Methuen Playscripts

Paul Ableman	TESTS
Edward Bond	SAVED
Kenneth H. Brown	THE BRIG
David Campton	LITTLE BROTHER: LITTLE SISTER and OUT OF THE FLYING PAN
Henry Chapman	YOU WON'T ALWAYS BE ON TOP
David Cregan	THREE MEN FOR COLVERTON TRANSCENDING and THE DANCERS
John McGrath	EVENTS WHILE GUARDING THE BOFORS GUN

*   *   *   *   *

Other Plays from Methuen

Jean Anouilh	COLLECTED PLAYS VOLUME I (*The Ermine, Thieves' Carnival, Restless Heart, Traveller without Luggage, Dinner with the Family*) COLLECTED PLAYS VOLUME II (*Time Remembered, Point of Departure, Antigone, Romeo and Jeanette, Medea*)
Bertolt Brecht	PLAYS VOLUME I (*The Caucasian Chalk Circle, The Three-penny Opera, The Trial of Lucullus, The Life of Galileo*) PLAYS VOLUME II (*Mother Courage, St Joan of the Stockyards, The Good Person of Szechwan*)
Max Frisch	THREE PLAYS (*The Fire Raisers, Count Oederland, Andorra*)
Jean Giraudoux	PLAYS VOLUME I (*Tiger at the Gates, Duel of Angels, Judith*) PLAYS VOLUME II (*Amphitryon, Intermezzo, Ondine*)
John Millington Synge	PLAYS AND POEMS